DEDICATION

To all the kind people I've met in digital spaces over the years … and look forward to meeting in the future. To my kids Xander and Ella Grace – thank you for your patience. See, I'm really working when I'm on the "tweeter thing."

Digital Kindness

being human in a
hyper-connected world

Lauren M. Hug

Published in the United States of America

Printed in the United States of America

ISBN: 978-1-948415-40-8

Library of Congress Control Number:2019907930

CONTENTS

ACKNOWLEDGMENTS

I talk about digital media and how it's changing us as humans pretty much all the time. My favorite thought partners and digital thinkers include: Regan Opel, Tillie Elvrum, Carrie Kintz, Matt Kaskavitch, and Micki Cockrille. Special thanks to Wendy Carson, my very first digital friend. Your dedication to community inspired me, and your hilarious commentary on life never fails to make me laugh.

FOREWORD

The Internet has radically transformed how we communicate, whether across the world or across the street. Silicon Valley has designed powerful tools that have reshaped the political and cultural landscape while providing space for endless hours of entertainment. But these digital platforms are just that — tools. They can be used for negative communication just as easily as positive.

So what are the rules of engagement? How should we behave? What morals guide us online? Aside from what our own character dictates, there are no rules. And we have all learned that anonymity can bring out the worst in people.

That's why digital kindness is one of the most significant challenges we face.

Social media is a convenient scapegoat. Some say it's tearing apart our social discourse, ruining children's ability to communicate face-to-face and fundamentally changing the outcome of a Presidential election. But all of this says more about us as a society than it does about technology.

Consider the automobile. It can take us to buy food at the grocery store or drive into a crowd of people. The user decides how to employ the tool. So why is social media seen differently? It's just as powerful and can have even more significant impacts.

Years ago, I was taught `no-look' computer keyboarding in high school. It was designed at the height of the dotcom era to introduce kids to the technology of the future. It's been two decades now. Technology has exploded in ways we could never have imagined and it's time to shift focus. We must use digital platforms more appropriately and responsibly. We've all mastered the keyboard, but what we do with it remains wild, untamed and often comes with unintended consequences.

One very positive and intended consequence of social media is my friendship with Lauren Hug. We met on Twitter following the destructive Waldo Canyon Fire, which burned neighborhoods in Colorado Springs — one of the worst natural disasters in city history. It's incredible how social media brought us together during such a trying time. We both used social media prolifically during the disaster to share accurate information with our community. Without Twitter, Lauren and I would have likely never crossed paths. Putting ourselves authentically in a digital space and showing kindness to one another spurred an everlasting connection.

Her timely and highly relevant book is all about putting your authentic self forward online, not some faux persona you wish you were. This book is a refreshing antidote to the often toxic online media landscape we all sadly inhabit. She asks readers to consider how they use digital platforms and to reflect on their digital behavior. This book should be required reading for every child in America.

It is full of useful exercises for children and adults alike. Lauren shares her unique personal experiences mixed with considerable expertise in communication to provide a hard look at today's digital environment. Where are we going wrong? Why do we behave differently in online spaces as compared to physical ones?

We're all media companies now. What we choose to broadcast via the Internet has a tremendous impact. Behind every online photo, video, status, tweet, 'gram, and pin is a human being. The more authentic the better. The sooner we learn to treat people online with the same respect and kindness that we use with people offline the better we will all be.

That will be a long journey, but this book provides a detailed road map on how to get there.

Matthew Kaskavitch
Director of Digital Engagement
University of Colorado Anschutz Medical Campus

LAUREN M. HUG

PREFACE

I love digital media. It's been a big part of my livelihood, but it's also my life. No exaggeration. Aside from my family, everyone – and I mean *everyone* I interact with in the real world on a daily basis are people I know because of social media connections.

In the summer of 2012 I planned a move from Austin to Colorado Springs. I didn't know a single soul in my adopted city, so I used Twitter to get answers to basic questions about living there. I found Twitter informative and entertaining — but, at that point, it was just a means to an end. I didn't see it as a powerful way of connecting humans and creating a better world.

I didn't see it as transformative.

Then the fire happened.

I was packing up my house in Austin when a fire swept through Colorado Springs. Roughly 32,000 residents were evacuated; 346 homes were destroyed. It consumed the very neighborhood where my new house was located.

From my sofa in Austin, Twitter connected me to Colorado Springs. It made me part of the community before I ever even lived there. And it enabled the entire city to unite in a common purpose.

Together we commiserated about the loss and devastation. Together we solved problems – crowdsourcing information about which houses had burned, where to find shelter, how to fill needs, how to support and honor the incredible firefighters who battled the blaze.

And when the ash settled, I was all in.

I belonged to Colorado Springs.

So I finished packing the truck and moved to a city where I knew no one and had no job waiting for me. I built an entire life – and business – from relationships formed on social media. Every one of my friends in Colorado Springs and all of my business can be traced directly back to Twitter.

I believe in the power of social media to unite humanity because I have experienced it firsthand. Social media can amplify generosity, mobilize compassion, and blanket the world with kindness.

But that's not how most of us use it every day. We rant. We complain. We argue. We forget there are human beings on the other side of the screen with different experiences, and different realities, who have different reactions to the things we post, the things we say, and the things we don't say. It's ugly out there in the digital world ... and that ugliness is spilling out into the real world.

It's time to change that.

I believe we can.

I believe the stakes are so high we have to.

Join me in exploring *digital kindness* as a way of being human in a hyper-connected world.

Lauren M. Hug

1
WHY DIGITAL KINDNESS MATTERS

People love to complain about the downsides of digital media. There is always some new study about how it ruins relationships, destroys civil discourse, gives rise to "fake news," impacts our sleep cycles, causes people to become depressed or anxious, and puts additional pressure on teens to conform and pander for "likes." But much of the negativity about digital activity seems to assume that we are — and have no choice but to be — passive consumers of this technology.

I have a different view. I believe social media gives us unprecedented power to explore our world and the incredible complexity, beauty, and breadth of humanity in countless ways. It can make us more aware, more understanding, more effective, and more *human*. It can bring us together rather than drive us apart. Heal instead of hurt ...

If we choose to use it that way.

How many people can you connect with in a lifetime? For previous generations — those that lived before innovations in transportation and communication — the number was relatively small. Connections were limited to a circle of immediate family, friends, and others living and working within the same physical community. Exposure to ideas and life experiences outside of the small circle came at an arm's-length — through letters, periodicals, and books, and later through radio, television, and film. Outside voices didn't often invade everyday life with an immediacy and relevance that demanded attention.

Digital communication has vastly expanded our ability to connect with people far beyond our families, friends, and physical communities. It connects us with an increasing number of strangers every day. Social media puts the stories, images, and thoughts of outsiders and people we barely know alongside those of our most cherished loved ones.

We read the thoughts of strangers in the comments sections of online publications. We're exposed to people we don't know through discussions on a friend's Facebook, Instagram, or blog post. We constantly open ourselves up to commentary and perspectives from people we've never met (and will probably never meet in person) when we use Twitter or Instagram or YouTube or any number of other "public" social media channels.

How are we to navigate interactions with these outsiders who are becoming a very real and hard-to-ignore presence in our daily lives? How should we behave toward those who

2

enter our lives through digital means — both those who say and do things that hurt or infuriate us as well as those we seem to connect with and bond with quickly? Are these digital connections *real*? Should we treat them as real people with real lives or is it okay to treat them as fictional characters because we don't encounter them in physical spaces?

Digital communication also shows us different sides of those we already know. How should we react when family, friends, and those we know in one specific context (work, the gym, a shared hobby, etc.) say or do something in a digital space that shocks us, hurts us, worries us, or causes us to reevaluate our relationship with them? Should we call them out publicly? Interact with them privately? Or sever ties completely?

"Social media has become such an integrated component of human interaction," says Brian A. Primack, M.D., Ph.D, Director of the University of Pittsburgh's Center for Research on Media, Technology, and Health. "It's important ... to recognize the balance to be struck in encouraging potential positive use, while redirecting from problematic use."

Since the dawn of digital communication, we've been consuming social media without much reflection on how it impacts us, how it changes the way we interact, and how it changes what we know about people (both friends and strangers). But digital media has matured. It has been around long enough for us to stop passively consuming and mindlessly reacting and start using it in purposeful and thoughtful ways. We can educate ourselves, protect ourselves, connect with others, and create positive impact in our communities and the larger world.

It's time to be purposeful about our digital behavior — harnessing its power for good and being conscious of the ways it causes harm.

It's time to practice **digital kindness.**

With the click of a button we can communicate instantly with someone on the other side of the planet — someone we would never encounter through other means. We can "get to know them" on their terms, observing their life through the stories and photos they choose to share on social media channels. We can see what matters to them. How they think. What they are experiencing.

Social media breaks down barriers by allowing us to see the common threads that unite humanity — love, joy, excitement, triumph, grief, pain, loss, fear. Real lives are on display all across the digital world — and we can learn a lot by using it to *see, listen,* and *connect.*

Social media gives us unprecedented opportunity to have a positive impact one-to-one, locally, and even globally by being purposeful about our digital behavior. When we are *thoughtful* and *honest* in digital spaces, we can forge meaningful relationships, engage in constructive dialogue, and crowdsource custom solutions. We can build communities that transcend cultures, borders, and languages.

We *can* use social media this way. But that's not how most of us choose to use it.

Instead of building bridges and connections with others, we tend to use social media to focus on ourselves — our views, our perspectives, our grievances. We sometimes forget there are human beings on the other side of the screen ... or we simply don't think about the impact our posts could have on those with different lives, different realities, and different ideas.

Social media lacks context and social cues, leading us to extremes we would avoid when interacting in person. This thoughtless, careless approach to social media is causing real harm in the real world.

Digital kindness begins with a commitment to embracing positivity. I'm not talking about forced smiles or an overly chipper outlook. I'm not recommending a steady broadcast of inspirational quotes. Embracing positivity simply means choosing to communicate in a friendly and upbeat way. It means going out of our way to demonstrate goodwill, assume positive intent, and act with care, and concern for fellow human beings.

Committing to positivity also means *not* using social media to routinely vent, argue, or contribute to ugliness. None of us is perfect, and we'll all have a day here or there where we see social media as our best outlet for expressing strong opinions or emotions, but perpetually engaging in angry, heated, long-winded rants is not kind.

Angry, heavy-handed, one-sided posts don't build solid relationships and foster understanding. They fan the flames of frustration and discontent, reinforcing feelings of hopelessness and despair. No one is going to change their mind about *anything* because of some argument on social media. Perhaps, more importantly, we may never even know how many people saw the argument and decided to never engage with us (or the other participants) again. *Civil* discourse, on the other hand, can go a long way toward establishing common ground and understanding.

Digital kindness provides a framework for interacting with friends and strangers in ways that benefit both them and us. It enables us to forge authentic connections in a world of virtual reality. It protects us from the real hurt caused by thoughtless digital behavior. It results in real friendships that add richness and diversity to our lives. It's something we can practice every day.

Together, we can transform digital spaces into kinder places.

Chapter 1 Questions

- How do you feel about social media?

- How do you usually use social media?

- What networks do you use most?

- What kinds of things do you usually post?

- How do you interact with others on social media?

- How often do you interact with people you haven't met in real life? How do you tend to interact with them?

Chapter 1 Activities

- Map your social media activity for the past week. Use one color to highlight activity you see as positive (things that contributed positively to your life). Use another color to highlight activity you see as negative (things that made you feel anxious, upset, or other unpleasant emotions).

- Make a plan to increase your positive social media activity next week.

- Re-think the negative social media activities from last week. Brainstorm ways to transform them into positive activities or ways to avoid negative emotions.

LAUREN M. HUG

2
KINDNESS SEES

Intentional or not, our daily routines keep us locked inside boxes. We see the same people. We talk about the same things. We naturally gravitate toward people who look, live, and think a lot like us.

That's one of the biggest reasons formal education has traditionally focused so heavily on the humanities. Studying how human beings throughout time and across cultures have defined a good and meaningful life combats the stagnation and closed thinking that accompanies our tendency to stick with what we already know.

"Literature and the arts enable us to see through a new lens, to look at the world through others' eyes," says Harvard University President Drew Faust. "We learn, for example, how civilizations have varied across space and time. We come to understand that the world has been different and could and will be different again."

Philosophy, literature, religion, art, music, history, and language are all ways we express our humanity. Exploring these subjects encourages critical thinking, fosters creative problem solving, deepens our understanding of the world, and helps us build toward a better, more inclusive, and more innovative future. These subjects help us see past who we are and where we come from — beyond the world we were born into and beyond the world we encounter every day — to appreciate the breadth of humanity. They show us all the things we have in common with those who, at first glance, appear vastly different from ourselves. They acquaint us with different answers, different solutions, and different ways of living that can challenge and enrich our own lives.

Books, movies, television shows, and the arts are common ways we are introduced to ideas and people vastly removed from our daily existence. They have the potential to humanize those we overlook, ignore, and despise. They raise our awareness of populations or issues we don't think impact us ... and show us how we are all connected or why we should care. They enable us to empathize with people going through something we otherwise couldn't imagine. They make us more capable of seeing things from other people's perspectives.

There is a problem, however, with using books, movies, and television and art as a window into experiences and thoughts different from our own. These windows are limited by the authors, artists, patrons, distributors and gatekeepers. Which stories are worthy of being shared? Which ideas are worthy of spreading? Which cultures are worthy of being explored? Throughout history, a select few

people have had the power and influence to decide —
based on their own experiences, preferences, education,
and interests — what other people should see, hear, and
learn. Many voices have been overlooked, silenced, ignored,
or deemed unimportant.

Even autobiographies, songs, or works of art created
without any external direction have a filter attached to
them. They have been edited, condensed, and fixed to be
more presentable. They're not as raw as real-time
communications and interactions that occur on a daily
basis. They rarely come from the perspective of someone
currently experiencing the situation.

Digital media gives us the ability to see people as they
are — or as they choose to present themselves — in *real
time*. Unedited. Often unfiltered. Social media opens us up
to a new way of seeing past political, professional,
philosophical, cultural, and socio-economic divides. It allows
us to see the world directly through the eyes of our fellow
human beings. It lets us see things from the perspective of
normal people, not just those with money, power, access,
or prestige. And it enables us to see how much they are like
us ... or we are like them.

Every person on social media is voluntarily starring in
their own reality show.

And, unlike the highly edited, highly produced reality
shows that have taken over television, the social media
activity of normal people doesn't suffer from a lack of
diversity, creativity, or compelling plots. Real life is full of
comedy, drama, and everything in between. Spend enough
time on social media, and you'll see: the truth is stranger
and more interesting than fiction.

Digital media has swept the gatekeepers aside, giving anyone with a computer or smartphone the power to publish their stories and ideas. We now have the ability to experience the world with our fellow human beings through countless blogs, status updates, tweets, and snaps. Digital platforms like YouTube and the rise of live-streaming via Facebook, Instagram, and other apps has put the power of video into nearly everyone's hands. Anyone can create a film, produce their own show, or share with the world whatever they are seeing and experiencing in real time. And anyone with a computer or a smartphone can witness these personal and often real-time stories.

We can walk down the streets of Calcutta with someone who truly knows every aspect of the city and navigates those streets every day. We don't have to wonder how much is being edited out by a film-maker with an agenda. We get to see what matters to a specific individual — a real person. On Twitter, a physician diagnosed with terminal cancer shared her experiences with end-of-life care. With a sense of humor and technical expertise, she opened eyes to both the medical and human side of the difficult to discuss but universal issue of dying. On Facebook Live one woman brought joy to the world with a Chewbacca mask and an infectious laugh, while another exposed racism and police brutality by live-streaming the aftermath of the fatal shooting of her boyfriend.

Social media gives us an immediate connection with people we would never encounter otherwise. We can have real-time experiences and conversations with people who live anywhere. The only barrier is our own willingness to explore the world in this way.

Many of the people I interact with on social media are people I can't imagine meeting in any other way. Without Twitter, I never would have met my friend Wendy. Our natural social circles are different. Our politics (and views about discussing politics) are very, very different. I doubt our non-digital paths would ever have crossed. But social media allowed us to see all the things we have in common: a devotion to our children, community involvement, and a commitment to seeing, hearing, and caring for the people we encounter. It also allowed our personalities to shine through. Wendy is one of the funniest people I know. Her tweets make me snort with laughter and her witty observations about current events, television shows, and her own life never fail to brighten my day — even when I disagree with her views and arguments. I cannot imagine my world without her. The core values we share and the compatibility of our temperaments far outweigh any conflicts or disagreements.

And I'm thankful we don't agree on everything. Knowing her helps me see things from another perspective. When she voices an opinion I think is wrong, I can't dismiss her as stupid or mean or evil. I can't be angry about her position. She's my friend. A person I love. A person who strives for the good of those around her. I can't easily dismiss her view. I have to process it and consider it on a deeper level than the opinions of those I don't know or respect. Grappling with her perspective refines my own opinions and challenges me to look for common ground.

Interactions on social media force us to look beyond simple labels and view people as complex beings. When we see someone's vacation photos, wedding photos, birthday celebrations, expressions of grief at losing someone they loved — their gender, race, religion, nationality, profession, or age doesn't really matter. Those feelings of love and joy and loss and pain are universal. When we can *feel* along with someone else, we can start to see the world differently.

Unfortunately, most social media usage is self-focused. Instead of using digital media to see others, we tend to use it to gaze at ourselves. In discussing the "ills" of social media in regards to adolescents, Christine Rosen, senior editor of *New Atlantis: A Journal of Technology & Society,* said the "immediate and chronic danger is its tendency to encourage teens constantly to compare themselves to their peers."

Does social media actually *encourage* people to compare themselves to others? Or is that simply how most of us have chosen to use it?

Digital kindness takes the focus off of us and how we compare to others. It encourages us to use social media to truly see others. And not just snapshots and glimpses. Digital kindness is a commitment to seeing people as *more* than their social media posts or bios.

When we don't *see* people, it's easy to say and do things that hurt. It's easy to be hurt by things they say and do. It's easy to assume the worst, and to put people in boxes where they don't really belong.

People are complicated, messy, inconsistent, idiosyncratic, and interesting. No one is all good or all bad … or all one thing or another. If we look closely enough, there's *something* to like, admire, or value about every person.

I realize that's a controversial statement. How can there

possibly be anything to like about a person who seems to despise, hate, or fight against values, rights, and experiences we hold dear? How can we see them as *more* than the opinions they express?

Seeing people via social media prevents us from vilifying those who are different from us. It reminds us that people are multi-faceted with multiple and conflicting characteristics, interests, and, yes, prejudices.

It's possible — even likely — for a person to say vile and hateful things in one breath and helpful, healing things in another. The person who disagrees with us most loudly on politics may be the only person who brings soup when we're sick. In a world that seems to be becoming more and more polarized, it's important to recognize an enemy on one issue may be a strong ally on another. Just because we can't see eye to eye on one topic doesn't mean we're on opposing sides of all topics … or that we can't find some common ground somewhere.

When we're upset, frustrated, or confused about an issue, digital media lets us quickly and easily find a person — another human being — who thinks the same, the opposite, or something we've never considered before. It gives us the chance to ask them *why*. We can learn their reasons, and recognize that their life is bigger and more expansive than this one opinion or viewpoint.

To be kind in digital spaces, we must pay attention to what people are posting, and, sometimes, look past what they are posting — look past images and memes and headlines and rants — to see a complex and whole being. We must choose to see a human being worthy of being treated with dignity and respect … whether we like that person or agree with that person, or not.

Seeing the complexity of how people approach issues gives us a better understanding of how to heal wounds, build bridges, and find mutually beneficial solutions. Digital kindness takes the time and makes the effort to see the humanity of everyone we encounter in social media spaces.

Chapter 2 Activities

- How many people in your life have very different views or backgrounds from you?

- How do you typically respond to people who are different from you?

- Who do you follow or interact with most on social media? People you already know in real life or people you've met online?

- Has social media opened your eyes to a viewpoint, lifestyle, or experience different from what you've encountered before? How?

- Do you believe social media can build bridges and foster positive relationships? Why or why not?

Chapter 2 Activities

- Make a list of books, television shows, movies, plays, and other works of art that have changed your perception about something. Reflect on why each item impacted you.

- Finish this statement 3 times: "I can't believe anyone could ever think _____." Find at least one person on social media who thinks that way. Spend a week seeing what else that person thinks and shares.

LAUREN M. HUG

3
KINDNESS CONNECTS

People use social media because they want to be seen. We post on social media networks because we want someone to pay attention. We're looking for connection and interaction. When we don't get a response — when no one likes or comments on our posts — we feel ignored, unimportant, or bewildered.

In the last chapter we talked about ways to truly *see* people via social media. But digital media gives us unprecedented ability to interact with people too. Digital kindness acknowledges the existence of others in a positive and productive way. Kindness in digital spaces means letting people know we see them.

Digital kindness *connects*.

And it's incredibly easy to do.

Say hello.

Ask friendly questions.

Rejoice with those who are celebrating.

Mourn with those who are grieving.

Show concern and care for anyone who is lonely, hurting, or afraid.

It's that simple. A few words of acknowledgment in digital spaces mean a lot.

Taylor Swift is excellent at using social media to connect with fans in positive and meaningful ways. She is known for visiting Instagram accounts and leaving comments on photos. She says positive, encouraging, supportive, and *specific* things about the photo or the person. Imagine being an awkward, marginalized fourteen- or fifteen-year-old who finds a comment from TAYLOR SWIFT on your Instagram post. Think about what it would feel like to know that one of the most famous, popular, and successful women in the world thought enough about you to leave an edifying, encouraging, personal message on your account. Think about what it would mean to every kid at your school who saw that comment.

It makes a huge difference! Who cares what bullies and mean kids say or think if TAYLOR SWIFT finds you valuable and important?

We're not all Taylor Swift, but taking the time to encourage and support someone definitely makes a difference. It makes the slings and arrows of daily life sting a little less. It makes it easier to laugh off negative criticism or ugly comments. It lifts moods. It makes a difference in how a person feels about themselves. It makes a difference in how a person interacts with others.

Choosing to connect with people in digital spaces lets people know they are worthy of acknowledgment ... worthy of someone's time ... worthy of someone's attention. It lets people know they matter.

Digital kindness is more than clicking the "like" button. Kindness speaks. It says, "I see you. I hear your story. I hear what you are saying. You are not alone."

When someone expresses sadness, loneliness, worthlessness, hopelessness, or even anger in digital spaces, they are often telling the world – in one way or another – that they don't feel seen, heard, or valued. It takes so little of our time and energy to say ...

I am sorry you are having a bad day.

I am sorry you have lost someone you love.

I am sorry your work situation is difficult.

I am sorry people are treating you badly.

I'm sorry you are scared and confused.

I am sorry you are feeling alone.

You are not alone.

Your feelings matter. Your experiences matter. Your pain matters.

YOU MATTER.

One day on Facebook, I saw a young man I had worked with making some comments that worried me. He sounded depressed and hopeless … potentially even suicidal. The comments could have been run-of-the-mill grousing, but how many times have we heard about someone doing something drastic and found countless clues *after the fact* in their social media activity?

I never want to be the person who saw the desperation and frustration and didn't even offer a kind word.

His comments were worrisome enough to me that I popped onto private messenger and said, "Are you OK?" Almost immediately, he responded with a flood of words about what was going on in his life. He was truly feeling lost, sad, and alone. He felt like there was no one in his regular circle of friends he could talk to about what he was experiencing. When none of his friends responded to his vague Facebook posts, he felt even more alone. He wanted someone to talk to him. He wanted someone to check in and see how he was doing. But he didn't know how to start a direct conversation about a topic that was incredibly difficult for him to process and discuss.

At the first sign of kindness, he poured out his story. He was so relieved to have someone listen to him. He was relieved to know that someone cared. It's not that his friends *didn't* care, he simply didn't have the words to express what he needed from them – and they weren't picking up on the signals he was sending.

It happens all the time.

A lot of us aren't very good at saying, "I need someone to listen to me. I need someone to show me they care." (I'm terrible at it. The *last* thing I ever want to do is appear needy or anything less than completely self-sufficient.) So we go about getting attention through a variety of ineffective means.

On digital channels people talk because they want somebody to talk back to them. Period. No one is sending questions and statements out into cyberspace in the hopes they get completely ignored. People say things because they want someone to respond.

Digital kindness responds.

It breaks my heart every time I see a sad statement — a statement of loss or pain or confusion or frustration — and there's no response from anyone. I always wonder, why hasn't anyone responded? All it takes is a kind word. An acknowledgment of the person's existence, experience, and feelings. A positive, uplifting, encouraging sentiment. A handful of words. An emoji, gif, or meme. Anything that says, *I see you and you matter* can make a world of difference.

There are so many ways we can do this!

Several years ago, a young woman used Twitter to process her feelings about her unplanned pregnancy. That's a situation with the potential to elicit vastly different reactions from people – both positive and negative. Thankfully, I didn't see any negativity. (It could have been there, but it didn't cross my feed.) I *did* see two of my friends rally around this young woman ... assuring her she was being heard and that people were there for her. All they said was, "We know this is tough. We're here for you if you need to talk." There was no judgement. No overbearing advice. Just connection and kindness.

This young woman decided to go through with the pregnancy, and the digital connection forged as she was processing her options turned into real life relationships. These Twitter pals went from sharing kind words and a listening ear to providing her with cribs and car seats and baby clothes and play dates.

I see you. I'm here for you. I care about you. You matter.

It's so powerful. The digital world gives us a space where *anyone* can voice their concerns, their fears, their loss and *anyone* can say *I see you and you matter*. The effort it takes is minimal, but the impact of letting people know you see them and think them worthy of your time and attention is huge. The exchanges may be small, brief, and simple, but they mean the world to somebody who thinks they are alone.

Flying by myself to Arkansas for my grandma's funeral, I tweeted about where I was going and why. I received so many kind and uplifting responses from people I barely know. Comments about the specialness of grandparents and how hard it is lose them. People sending me condolences. People wishing me comfort, joy, and peace. The digital chorus of kind voices and thoughts and prayers were my companions on a difficult journey. The statements were small and brief, but they meant that my grief was seen and heard. That there were people who understood. There were people who cared enough about me to take a few moments out of their day to acknowledge my loss. It made me feel like I mattered.

In contrast, I never publicly posted about what I was experiencing as I was going through a divorce. While I know I have several friends — and am undoubtedly connected to countless strangers — who could and would provide emotional support throughout that process, I kept my feelings and experiences to myself. And I felt desperately, miserably, hopelessly alone most of the time. For me, *not* talking on social media about something I was going through made me feel isolated and inauthentic.

Everyone will approach digital sharing in different ways. No one should ever feel compelled to share something they aren't comfortable talking about publicly — no matter how much it may help someone else. But when someone opens up in social media spaces, digital kindness takes the time to connect. It goes beyond clicking a "like" button and proactively considers ways we can make somebody's day brighter. It takes very little time and effort on our part, but it has a tremendous impact for the individual ... and it ripples out into the world.

Connection creates positivity. It creates happiness. It creates community. And we cannot dismiss the fact that it very well may save lives.

When somebody is at the point where they no longer feel seen — where they don't feel like they add value to the world — even one small voice saying *you matter* can make the difference.

"I felt like I couldn't fix it," a 13-year-old victim of sexting told the Washington Post. "Like I was alone and nothing was ever going to be better."

Just a few kind words from anyone who has survived the horrors of junior high could make a difference. Reminders that life does go on after even the most embarrassing adolescent experience. Encouragement that this girl is not defined by a handful of photos. Affirmations of worth and value. It's not surprising the girl found refuge in the Minecraft community — a digital space where bullying, name-calling, and swearing are not allowed.

Start thinking about the ways you can connect with people in digital spaces. How can you add value to someone's life? What needs can you fill? How can you brighten someone's day and bring a smile to their face?

It's okay to start small. Start by making the effort to be kind to one person in one digital space every day. A kind word, a friendly emoji, an Instagram smile can brighten someone's day. Soon you'll find yourself being kind to two, five, 20 people a day.

Any time of day or night, *someone* is out there in cyberspace. *Someone* is listening. Be the someone who connects. Be the someone who lets people know you see them, you're there, you're listening, and you care.

Chapter 3 Questions

- How do you feel when no one likes or comments on one of your social media posts?

- How do you feel when someone comments on your post (instead of just "liking" it)?

- How often do you comment (instead of just "liking") people's posts?

- What experiences can you share that might be helpful to people looking for support, advice, or encouragement in digital spaces?

- Do you believe acknowledging someone in a digital space can make a difference in their life? Why or why not?

Chapter 3 Activities

- Make a list of simple phrases you can use to let people know you see them and care about them.

- Keep a record of every kind comment you make in digital spaces. Document the responses you receive. Document how the responses make you feel.

LAUREN M. HUG

4
KINDNESS LISTENS

Social media gives us the opportunity to see how similar we are to people who may appear to be very different from us. It allows us to connect and communicate with those we might not ever meet through our daily routines and normal lives. It opens our eyes to the things we have in common. But it also gives us the opportunity to learn about how and why we differ.

One of the most profound acts of kindness — one that is far too rare these days — is to listen, without judgement or agenda.

We live in a world of talkers — 24/7 people are talking on television, radio, and digital media. Words, words, and more words are spilled through blogs, status updates, and *content*.

With so many people talking, who's listening?

And when we listen, who are we listening to?

In this digital world, we have the unprecedented ability to listen to all kinds of voices on every topic imaginable. We have access to a wide variety of thoughts and perspectives. Yet we tend to listen to voices and perspectives that reflect and echo our own.

Instead of expanding our sources of information, we narrow them to those that reinforce the things we already think and believe. Even if we aren't intentionally seeking out like-minded voices, algorithms for social networks like Facebook and Twitter tend to feed us content that appeals to the preferences and viewpoints we already hold.

When we repeatedly encounter the same thoughts and ideas, we find ourselves surprised, perplexed, and even angry when confronted with a different perspective. We don't always know how to make sense of alternative or opposing views. There is a tendency to think that people who disagree with us are wrong or evil or out to hurt us. We don't see them as human. We see them as monsters. We develop an "us versus them" mentality. We feel the need to defend our position, prove the other side wrong, and argue people into agreeing with us.

Everyone wants to be heard, respected, and understood. And everyone has a really good case why they should get to speak first. Very few people are willing to listen and try to understand someone else.

It leaves us at an impasse.

Someone has to listen first.

In the name of digital kindness, let it be us.

Commit to listening to those who are different from you and those you disagree with. Strive to understand their reasons.

There is a story behind every belief or viewpoint a person holds. The story is always more interesting, more rich, more revealing than the belief or viewpoint itself. There is a collection of experiences and encounters and lessons that inform each opinion and position. Those experiences, encounters, and lessons tell you far more about a person than the boxes they check on a ballot, the bumper stickers they put on their car, or the ways they choose to spend their free time.

If we're willing to listen.

Social media lets us listen to the reasons behind a viewpoint. It lets us examine the experiences that inform perspectives. It humanizes philosophies and ideologies. And a humanized perspective is a lot harder to dismiss.

When we are willing to listen to the personal, experiential, *human* reasoning behind an opposing viewpoint, it becomes a lot harder to assume bad intent. It becomes lot harder to decide there's nothing of value or worth in a position ... or to say that no reasonable, responsible, or *good* person could think that way.

When we listen, we start to understand that the same desires for security, comfort, love, joy, and meaning underlie most ideas. We start to see we simply have different ways of prioritizing what matters or different ways of achieving similar outcomes.

When we feel like we know someone, we are more open to seeing the world through their eyes. We're more interested in solutions that take their concerns into consideration. We're more willing to try to understand why they speak, act, and think the way they do. And the more *someones* we get to know, the more collaborative, creative, and inclusive we instinctively become.

Digital media provides a safe space to listen and ponder different views. We don't have to walk into places that scare us or places where we don't feel welcome. We can follow people from different backgrounds and perspectives. We can watch a variety of human experiences from the comfort of our home. We can start conversations with a wide variety of people from our own sofa. We can make connections before we ever meet someone in person ... so when we do meet in real life, we know each other already. It's like getting together with an old friend.

Speaking of friends and social media ... it may actually be easier to commit to listening to strangers than to friends and family who express views on social media that surprise us. Our friends are usually people with whom we share at least one key commonality. It may be a shared workplace, passion, interest, or belief — but whatever it is, that common ground often leads us to think we have much more in common with our friends than may actually be true.

Social media often reveals aspects of our friends and family that we never see outside the digital realm. Unless someone is meticulous about managing privacy settings and permissions on each and every one of their social media accounts, their posts are a hodgepodge of various aspects of their life, interests, and views.

Posts about work mingle with posts about leisure activities.

Posts about relationships mix with posts about politics.

Posts about projects or passions mix with shares of the

latest BuzzFeed article, meme, or easy recipe.

Social media reveals things about our friends' views that may have never come up organically in conversation. (Or things they may deliberately avoid when chatting in person with us — because they know where we stand, and don't want to have a discussion with us about that topic.)

It's jarring to discover someone we think is on the same page as us holds different or opposing opinions on issues we feel strongly about. We don't always know how to respond when we encounter a friend's true feelings on a topic.

An increasingly common response is to publicly confront, chastise, or call out the person on social media ... or to publicly challenge anyone who disagrees on a particular issue to "unfriend" or "unfollow" us. This approach is damaging family relationships and life-long friendships on a daily basis.

Instead of publicly voicing disagreement or engaging in social media arguments, take the time to truly listen and consider other points of view. Ponder their words. Read the links they post. Watch the videos they share. Observe their real-time responses to current events. Commit to listening without judgment or agenda. Listen to understand, instead of searching for flaws and errors. Listen to find common ground, instead of fodder for the next debate.

Listening goes a step beyond seeing and connecting. Listening embraces a willingness to examine our own assumptions, beliefs, and ideas in response to the views of others. It's a willingness to explore the world from a different perspective ... and with an open mind. It's a willingness to see through the eyes of another.

"Everybody believes they are the good guy," says former CIA officer Amaryllis Fox, based on her experience in counterintelligence. "If you hear them out, if you're brave enough to really listen to their story, you can see that more often than not, you might have made some of the same choices, if you'd lived their life instead of yours."

When we recognize that no one sees themselves as a villain ... when we acknowledge that people think their own views are true and right and good ... when we accept that, from their perspective, their experiences, their reality, these beliefs and actions *are* right and good ... and when we make room for the possibility that, if we'd had those same experiences, we might believe the same things and take the same actions too ... we are on the path to understanding.

When we listen with an open mind, we are on the path to finding common ground far beyond our basic and shared humanity. We may discover ways of getting past whatever roadblocks and barriers are preventing us from working together towards mutually-agreed upon goals. We may be able to find the places where we are allies instead of enemies.

Listening builds trust.

It strengthens relationships.

It increases empathy.

It lays the foundation for a community that transcends ideologies and identities.

Digital kindness listens.

It resists the urge to talk or prove or argue.

It resists the urge to dismiss ideas and experiences different from our own.

Listen for a long time before talking.

Listen and earn respect.

Listen and build credibility.

If you want *your* words to be heard, listen first. People listen to those who listened to them.

Chapter 4 Questions

- Do you tend to talk more or listen more? Do you behave differently in person than you do online?

- Do you listen to understand? Or do you listen to argue and make your point?

- Has hearing about another person's experience ever changed your point of view? When and why?

- Do you believe people can hold truly awful views and still be worthy of compassion – or even friendship? Why or why not?

- How do you currently respond to friends who post things you strongly disagree with? Why is that the way you choose to respond?

- Have you ever publicly "unfriended" someone or invited people to "unfriend" you? Why or why not?

Chapter 4 Activities

- Make a list of news sources, bloggers, friends, etc. who you tend to listen to most. Rate them on a scale of 1-10. 1 = "We disagree on everything." 10 = "We agree on everything." Note how much diversity of thought exists among the people you follow.

- Make an effort to notice all the types of people or viewpoints you have difficulty understanding. Pick one and spend several weeks listening (via digital media) to a person from that group or viewpoint.

- Develop a personalized plan for responding to friends who post things that anger, upset, or disappoint you. Consider what matters to you most: speaking your mind, keeping the peace, pointing out a different perspective, changing someone's mind, etc.

5
KINDNESS IS THOUGHTFUL

Social media allows us to see, connect, and listen like never before ... but it's also a confusing, jumbled mess. An inside joke follows news of a bombing. A vacation photo is wedged between a store closing and a celebrity sighting. The fake news outlets look almost as legitimate as the real news outlets. Family members, life-long friends, business associates, new acquaintances, and complete strangers mix and mingle in the same digital spaces.

In real life, when speaking one-on-one or in small groups, we have some sense of who we are talking to, and the context of the conversation is clear to everyone involved. As a conversation progresses, we naturally pick up on social cues adapting our tone, words, body language, and facial expressions to suit our conversation partners. Most of us don't swear in places of worship or in front of our grandparents. We don't talk to family members in exactly the same way we talk to friends. We tend to avoid certain topics with certain people. We know not everyone we interact with thinks the same way.

We instinctively communicate differently when speaking to large groups of people — especially when a group is diverse and doesn't share many characteristics. Most of us tend to be more careful about the words we choose, the jokes we tell, or the examples we cite. We try to be as inclusive, neutral, and universal as possible when addressing large audiences.

Because of this never-ending interconnectivity of digital spaces, posting on social media is like speaking to a stadium full of people. Everything we post has the potential to reach countless folks. And while a post may not reach millions, it will undoubtedly reach someone we never thought about while creating it.

It *will* reach someone we forgot was following us. Someone we don't know at all. Someone we assume is on the same page with us, but who actually sees the world very differently. It *may* reach our boss, our ex, our kindergarten teacher, or our kids. No matter what privacy settings we use, sharing and screenshotting mean we have no control over who eventually sees our post.

Yet we tend to post as though only a handful of close friends will see our photos and our thoughts.

What about the people we didn't consider when posting something?

What about the people we know and love who are going through a tough time?

What about our treasured family and friends who hold

different political, religious, or lifestyle views?

What about co-workers and acquaintances who never knew what we thought about a particular issue, nor did it ever matter to them until it was shoved in their face? Too often, the people we forget, exclude, offend, or hurt don't tell us how our posts make them feel. One or two might voice displeasure or disagreement, but they are quickly shouted down by the many who agree with our position. They aren't likely to voice disagreement with us again.

In the vast, chaotic sea of people and content, it's not always clear who even the most innocuous comment was intended for ... who a post was directed at ... or what was meant by either. Lack of facial expressions, tone of voice, social cues, or sufficient context adds to the confusion. Misunderstandings abound. Tempers easily flare. With so much negativity in digital spaces, even the most mundane, simple statement runs the risk of being interpreted as a mean or snarky.

Digital kindness takes all this into consideration when choosing what to post and how to respond. To minimize miscommunication, hurt feelings, and broken relationships, we must be mindful of how context, the public nature of social media activity, and the lack of facial expressions, tone of voice, and visible reactions impact the ways in which we communicate with one another in digital spaces.

Consider Context

Using social media as an endless broadcast of our triumphs, complaints, worries, and opinions can impact our followers. If all we post are the good things that happen, followers may compare their own lives unfavorably to our highlight reel. If all we post are complaints or worries about the world, people may feel paranoid or anxious after reading our feed. If all we post are opinions, followers may feel offended, dismissed, or misunderstood.

Because many social media networks don't default to displaying posts in a chronological order (opting to display posts ordered by proprietary algorithms instead), things pop up in the middle of a feed without any indication of what prompted the post, what came before the post, or what comes after. Sometimes, the first post we see is the third statement in a series of five, so we don't immediately grasp the totality of what the person is saying or why they're saying it.

Digital rants tend to be responsive to something a person has recently seen or experienced — current events or personal situations we may not be aware of. We rarely know all the factors influencing a person's choice of words, tone, and posting frequency.

One of the kindest people I know surprised me by posting, "If you think my son comes from a shithole country, unfriend me now." The post came in the midst of controversy regarding one of President Trump's many inflammatory tweets about immigration. My friend is the adoptive mother of a beautiful child from Ethiopia. It stunned me to see a loving and compassionate person post something so angry and strident. I was aware of Trump's statement, of course, but nothing in my own newsfeeds merited that kind of impassioned response.

Turns out, however, that her feeds were full of hateful,

anti-immigrant rhetoric. And her feeds weren't the only ones. Another friend who had adopted a child from a "shithole" country felt the need to post something similar based on the ugliness she was seeing from people she knew and followed.

The way we encounter a post impacts how we perceive it. When a person posts every once in a while about their perfect relationship, political preference, or commitment to eating vegan, it's unlikely to bother us. If they post seven times in two hours about the same thing, it's bound to get on our nerves. If their posts also happen to appear amid a flood of other similar posts (say, on Valentine's Day, during an election cycle, or while a controversial topic is dominating both traditional media outlets and digital spaces) the effect can be overwhelming.

Lack of context (and unintended context) leads to misunderstandings and misinterpretations in digital spaces. It's easy to get angry or frustrated or be hurt or upset by something somebody says or does on social media. Given how often we experience these feelings ourselves when scrolling our feeds, it's important to consider whether our posts might make someone else feel the same negative emotions.

When I conduct seminars on digital kindness, everyone can list countless examples of digital behavior that offends or bothers them. When I ask whether they engage in some of the same behaviors, the room gets very quiet. We know what irks us, but we don't always think about what might irk others.

When interacting via social media, consider the limitations of digital spaces. Make a conscious effort to add whatever tone or context is necessary to ensure posts won't be perceived in a negative light. **Emojis are immensely helpful.** Punctuating a post with a wink or smile instantly infuses a flat statement with a sense of warmth and humor. Before clicking the "post", "tweet", or "share" button, reflect on how the post will be interpreted or perceived by others. How will it impact people with different experiences and lives from yours. Recognize that everyone will interpret a post through their own lens.

On National Siblings Day, my entire Facebook feed was filled with photos of brothers and sisters. It was the perfect opportunity to share a silly photo of me and my brother (circa ages 10 and seven) with bad haircuts, silly costumes, and goofy poses. My photo, like many others, made people laugh.

Other photos, though, were poignant tributes to siblings who had passed away. One friend shared a photo of his deceased brother, commenting that it was hard to see jubilant sibling photos because they reminded him of something he no longer had and desperately missed. Another friend shared how the photos made her sad because her daughter would never have a sibling. After a long and difficult struggle with infertility, it was unlikely she would ever have another child.

I'm fortunate to have a great relationship with my brother, and I've never experienced the range of emotions surrounding infertility. Before hearing their perspectives, it never occurred to me that a stream of sibling photos could cause someone pain.

A few years later, it was my turn to personally experience the pain of seeing social media flood with "happy photos" when I wasn't fortunate enough to be part of the "happy" crowd. The first holiday season after separating from my husband was brutal. I didn't have my kids for Thanksgiving (my favorite holiday), so the Facebook barrage of families and food broke my heart.

Because I live and breathe digital media for work, I've always been fairly thoughtful about what I post. That was the first time, however, that I fully understood on a personal level just how important the digital thoughtfulness I've been preaching for years really is.

I *did* have my kids for Christmas that year, and I thought long and hard before posting a few photos of us in front of our Christmas tree. I thought about how my photos might impact people feeling alone and lost. I thought about how photos captured in the few hours of genuine joy I felt during that miserable holiday season weren't an accurate depiction of the days of agony and despair I was enduring. I wondered about the level of transparency I owed to my digital network.

Ultimately, I decided to post three photos with a simple message: Merry Christmas.

There isn't one right answer to what to post and when. I cannot emphasize this enough. We all have different personalities, perspectives, and ways of expressing ourselves. Some things fill us with exuberance. Some things make us fume. Some things make us sad. We don't need to second-guess everything we ever post in the name of kindness. We don't need keep quiet on all holidays or avoid saying something about trending topics. But we should, at least, consider how our activity impacts others. And when we encounter a statement about pain, loss, anger, or fear in the face of a trend, we should respond with care and concern, *not* a dismissal of the person's feelings or an admonition to lighten up.

I try to be thoughtful about what I say and post on days when feeds will be flooded with a lot of similar content. Every time there's a trending topic about relationships, from siblings to parents to grandparents to significant others, I remind myself that someone I know and care about is going to feel left out. I try to acknowledge people whose situations prevent them from participating in the trending topic or whose life experiences make the topic painful or difficult. Those trending topics now prompt me to reach out to a friend who may be hurting because they don't belong in the trending category.

The more I've practiced this deliberate thoughtfulness, the more I've noticed how many people *don't* fit standard generalizations. For example, I started to realize Mother's Day was painful for some after my maternal grandmother passed away and my own mother expressed feeling a heightened sense of loss that day. Then I started to notice friends who struggled with infertility or who had endured a miscarriage sharing feelings of sadness surrounding the holiday. I slowly became aware of all sorts of people feeling left out or "less than" on Mother's Day. Women who had no desire to ever have children. People who were alienated from their mother for whatever reason. Single moms who had no partner to make the day special for them (a category I would later fall into myself).

There is no "one size fits all" experience. Thoughtful social media use reminds of us that.

I try to be aware of friends of who are conspicuously

silent on certain issues and various holidays. When a person who posts a lot is suddenly quiet, there's a good chance they're experiencing something too complex or painful for consumption by their entire digital network.

Likewise, when someone who is generally quiet on social media feels the need to speak up, I try to respect their courage and their passion. Something was obviously important enough to them to change their typical patterns of digital engagement.

When I'm the one hurting, I try to think about the degree to which I want to share my perspective and pain in the digital space — and how my digital activity might impact others. (I might actually think about this far too much, because I often stop myself from posting about my own experiences. And, as the next chapter discusses, sharing honestly about our experiences is another form of digital kindness.)

A post that surprises or shocks us is likely a response to things we aren't seeing or experiencing. Digital kindness looks for surrounding context to fully understand people's digital activity. Before commenting publicly, consider reaching out privately to a person to find out what motivated the post.

Digital kindness also provides as much context as possible to help prevent misunderstandings or hurt feelings. Embrace those emojis. Add an extra sentence of context or explanation. Think about an actual human you actually know who might be negatively impacted by your post. How can you soften the blow? How can rewrite it or reframe it to take their experience into consideration?

If you can't find a way to express your thoughts without

the realistic potential of hurting someone you know, consider whether those thoughts are really worth broadcasting across a digital space. Is this something *everyone* in the digital universe needs to see? Or is this something better reserved for smaller group discussions or in-person conversations?

There's no right answer to these questions. (I'll say this again and again.) But thinking about them will go a long way toward stemming the tide of unintentionally insensitive digital content.

Avoid Pressure

Remember the Ice Bucket Challenge? It was all over social media in the summer of 2014. Feeds were bombarded with videos of people dumping ice water on their heads. Huge numbers of celebrities got into the act. Former American Presidents even participated.

I, however, refused.

Not because I was anti-fundraising for ALS research, but because I'm opposed to pressuring anyone to do anything via social media. Frankly, I'm opposed to social pressure of almost any kind. I opt out of chain letters (remember those?), Facebook games, and any other activities that compel participation by calling people out or asking them to keep something going. I don't think it's OK when it happens in person ... and it's not OK when it happens in digital spaces.

I realize that the vast majority of people who participated in the Ice Bucket Challenge thought it was harmless fun for a good cause, but there's no denying a key component of the Challenge's unprecedented success was the use of social pressure. Calling somebody out publicly when that person doesn't want to be called out is not a nice thing to do.

During the Ice Bucket Challenge, several of my friends privately admitted they reluctantly participated because they felt like they "had to." While some may question why functional adults would feel compelled to participate in what is essentially a Facebook game for a good cause — Ice Bucket Challenge participants were former Presidents and successful businesspeople, not teens and tweens challenging each other to eat Tide Pods. We can't forget that several studies have revealed Facebook use makes many people feel inadequate and unsuccessful. Some researchers have even gone so far as to claim Facebook causes depression.

In other words, Facebook pressure is a real thing.

In the early days of the Ice Bucket Challenge, pressure to participate wasn't as high. The Challenge hadn't permeated pop culture yet, so ignoring it (the same way people ignore invitations to play Candy Crush or instructions to post a silly Facebook status) was a viable option. But once the Challenge was everywhere — and leaders of all kinds were playing along — there was a legitimate fear of being "the only one" unwilling to participate.

Because the Challenge occurred in social media spaces, there was no telling who would see you'd been called out. If you didn't respond by filming your soaking or announcing your generous donation to a charity, people might question your sense of humor, your compassion, and/or your generosity.

And that's not okay.

There are any number of reasons a person might have chosen not to participate in the Ice Bucket Challenge. Maybe they already made sizable donations to other worthy charities. Maybe they had a moral or religious objection to the type of research the funds would go to support. Maybe they weren't comfortable with the idea of broadcasting their charitable giving. Maybe they were simply self-conscious about being soaking wet on video. Whatever the reasons, no one should feel compelled to do something they aren't comfortable doing — and especially not because their friends and family are urging them to do it all because of a social media fad.

Please think before you publicly challenge people to participate in a social media trend. Just because you're fine with it doesn't mean somebody else is. How will a public call out make others feel? Ask yourself if you might make them uncomfortable by calling them out publicly. When in doubt, you can always just ask them before you name them in a social challenge ... or include language about how the challenge is meant to be fun and raise awareness and isn't intended to create pressure. If you insist on naming them publicly without asking them first, provide them with a gracious out.

If you've been called out yourself, remember it's always okay to say "no thanks". Everyone should feel free to ignore or opt out of any challenge or game without fear of repercussion. We should always be careful about judging a person because of their willingness or unwillingness to participate in a social media trend ... no matter how worthy the cause. That way, we can all rest assured that everyone is having fun and no one feels compelled to participate.

Be Respectful

You've probably been told at least once to "never talk about religion or politics" in the workplace … at a dinner party .. in polite conversation … during an interview … and in a zillion other situations. Given the pervasiveness of that advice — and the fact that most people more or less adhere to it in public conversations — it's astonishing how many people blather on about highly controversial topics in digital spaces. And *not* in pursuit of dialogue, either. Sometimes it seems as through strident, condescending, dismissive, insensitive, and tone-deaf statements about the most controversial and sensitive issues is the *only* content in digital spaces.

We seem to have adopted the idea that we aren't being true to ourselves and true to our beliefs if we don't talk about them often and loudly. In digital spaces, we don't have to look real people in the eyes, so it's easy to vilify the other side and do everything in our power to demonstrate why anyone from that camp is wrong or evil.

There's little room for kindness when we're busy passing judgment. Every day people are alienating friends, family, co-workers, and acquaintances because of their conduct in digital spaces — and most of the time we don't even realize it.

Not everybody connected to us via social media networks shares our beliefs on every topic. This may seem obvious, but I've lost count of the number of times friends have expressed anger, frustration, or shock at posts written by people they love and respect — posts they interpret as an indication the person doesn't love and respect them or their views.

We don't usually intend to offend or hurt others when we post strong opinions, but we often fail to consider how our posts might be viewed by someone with a different perspective. We forget that people from a wide variety of backgrounds, with a wide variety of opinions will see our social media posts. And without being able to see a person's physical reaction to our statements (a change in their facial expression or body language), the only way we'll ever know how our post made them feel is if they choose to tell us.

People pay far more attention to our social media posts than we often think — especially if the content relates to a topic important to them. They may not ever comment or express their thoughts about our digital activity, but they're reading and watching and forming an opinion in silence.

We may be the only representative from a particular viewpoint that a person knows. Are we expressing our strong opinions in a way that might persuade a person from a different perspective? Or are we preaching to the choir?

When we post about a strongly held belief, what are we trying to accomplish?

If we're hoping to change minds, using social media as a soapbox is misguided. People tend to feel attacked and compelled to defend their position — only deepening their commitment to that particular view. Others will disengage completely.

Too often, we assume silence means agreement. When a post gets a ton of "likes" and no one voices opposition, we tend to assume our position is much more popular amongst our network than it might actually be. In reality, a person who doesn't speak up or who chooses to stop arguing has most likely decided the conversation isn't worth having. Worse yet, they may have decided to stop listening to anything we have to say … and stop respecting our opinion altogether. Even people who agree may quietly fade away as well, because our tone and our approach makes them uncomfortable.

Because I am committed to seeing the world from a wide variety of perspectives, I almost never mute, block, or unfriend people. However, I have one friend who became so angry and one-sided for such an extended period of time (three years!), I decided I no longer wanted to see her posts in my feed. The funny thing is, I often agreed with her position. But the way she chose to express herself was so toxic and dismissive of others, I didn't want to deal with that negativity every day. I have no idea how she was conducting herself in real life at the time, because I hadn't been in the same physical space as her in many years. The picture she was painting of herself on Facebook, though, was angry and intolerant. I doubt she had any idea I muted her … or how many others did the same thing.

Instead of muting her, I wish I had practiced what I preach and connected with her privately to see what was motivating her angry posts. It was only when she reached out directly to me years later that I learned she had been in the midst of a nightmarish and life-altering experience. She was angry for a very good reason — and could have used my support, encouragement, and friendship. But, due to factors in my own life at the time, her digital activity alienated me. Thankfully, our friendship has been restored through direct communication.

During the 2016 Presidential election, another friend of mine posted "If you're even thinking about voting for [CANDIDATE X], unfriend me now and remove yourself from my life." Within a week of posting, he asked me to help him find a new job. It never occurred to him that his post might impact my impression of him or my willingness to tap my professional connections for his benefit. He never considered whether I intended to vote for that candidate, whether I have close friends and loved ones planning to vote for that candidate, or whether I simply disapprove of divisive statements in a digital space (something that should be fairly obvious to anyone who knows me even a little). He didn't think about how his post might impact the way prospective employers perceive him. He never considered the thoughts, feelings, or perceptions of anyone who sees the world differently from him. Unfortunately, the majority of his posts are so one-sided and unwelcoming to people of opposing viewpoints, very few who disagree with him will ever go to the effort of speaking up. He'll probably never know who he has offended or how many people have decided to distance themselves from him because of his digital activity.

"In 2016 there was a growing sense that people were losing their minds. And no one knew why ... until now." The opening scene of the 2016 CBS summer series *BrainDead*, a television show about brain-eating bugs from outer space making people more and more extreme, is funny, but also rings true. The 2016 election seemed to bring out the worst in many people — especially in digital spaces. Many people terminated friendships via Facebook due to conflicting political beliefs … or abandoned social media for long periods of time due to the discord.

However, most didn't end friendships or opt out of social media networks because of the political differences themselves; rather because of the way people expressed their political views on social media. Angry, mean-spirited posts that demean, criticize, and dismiss entire groups of people are hard to process for anyone who identifies themselves as part of the group. Reading those posts is bound to hurt a little, no matter how thick someone's skin. On one level, we may know our friend or acquaintance isn't directing their comments at us personally, but it's still hard to handle repetitive content questioning our morality or intelligence because we think a certain way.

And yet, we may be posting the same kind of content without realizing our posts bother people from opposing views in the same way their posts bother us. We share articles that categorize entire classes of people. We express frustration with those who don't act and think like us. We make sweeping, broad, and generalizing statements that fail to reflect nuances, subtleties, or exceptions.

We often don't even know when we're doing it. We get caught up in the likes, supportive comments, and shares of those who agree. Because so many of our social media pals express agreement, we start to believe we are "right". We become bolder and more one-sided in the things we post. And the social network algorithms reinforce our perception that most people agree with us. The algorithms show us more and more content we already "like".

As the 2016 Presidential election neared, I began asking my friends who they thought would win the election based on what they were seeing in their social media feeds. Without fail, people who identified with the political left thought Secretary Clinton was going to win by a healthy margin. Friends on the left reported not knowing *anyone* who was planning to vote for now-President Trump. Or, if they knew someone planning to vote for him, that person didn't count because that person was crazy.

There wasn't quite as much unanimity from my friends who identified with the political right. Some were from pockets that vehemently hated Trump and passionately believed he was not a true Republican. Those folks tended to think Clinton would win because posts in their newsfeeds showed a deep divide on right-wing support for Trump. Other friends from the right were confident Trump would win — either because their newsfeeds were full of enthusiastic support for him, full of hatred for Secretary Clinton, or a combination of both.

No one I talked to had spent a lot of time truly listening or paying attention to anyone from the other side. They didn't feel the need. Their newsfeeds — filled with the thoughts and perspectives of hundreds or even thousands of different people — told them everything they needed to know. The vast majority of people in their newsfeed more or less agreed with them.

And, since everyone in their feed agreed with them, they saw no problem with posting strident, loud, repetitive content reinforcing a position everyone already agreed with and dismissing (often unkindly and in very derogatory terms) other viewpoints.

But there *is* a problem with broadcasting *any* view or any content with little thought to how those views are articulated and how they might come across to people who think and believe differently. Regardless of how much agreement we *think* there is amongst our social media fans and followers, there is always at least one person — a person we deeply care about — who holds a different view.

It never occurs to many people that, unless they truly only knew people with a very specific set of views, they *must* know someone who holds a different view. We have to consider the possibility that our own social media activity can lead to friends with opposing views holding their tongue when interacting with us.

What good comes from using social media to pass judgment on opposing viewpoints, make public proclamations about who is and is not worthy of being a "friend" or "follower", or engage in public shaming or heated disagreements?

Think about one of your deeply held beliefs. Something central to your identity. A belief that defines who you are. Now think: what could someone post in a digital space that would make you change your mind? If we're being honest, the answer is probably *nothing*. If nothing can change *our* minds, why do we think our social media posts will convince others to change theirs? Especially when those posts drip with judgment, condemnation, contempt, and a complete insensitivity to the myriad reasons a person may hold a different view?

Digital kindness respects the sea of viewpoints comingling in digital spaces. When posting on social media think about communicating with someone from a different perspective instead of addressing the people who already agree with you. Save strong opinions for face-to-face conversations where you can respond appropriately to the social cues and emotional responses of all the people engaged in and listening to the discussion.

This all boils down to one very simple rule: **Think before you post!**

And this rule applies to everything you post. Even things you may think are innocuous.

In December of 2016, a click-bait titled video ("Did *you* spot the surprise?") circulated on social media. I saw it posted by several friends. Every time I saw it posted on Facebook, there were lots of "likes" and "wow" reactions.

When I first saw it, I was shocked. That's how I was supposed to feel. That's the reaction the video was aiming for. I wanted to share the video. It was a brilliant piece of content creation. It was thought-provoking and powerful.

But as I thought about clicking the "share" button, I started to sob. The intentionally disturbing nature of the video hit me hard … because I know someone who has lived through a situation similar to the one the video depicted. I wondered how they would feel if they encountered the video through my Facebook feed.

As soon as I thought of my friend, I knew I couldn't share the video without a trigger warning of some kind. I couldn't share the video without spoiling the "surprise" — because the "surprise" is exactly the problem for those who've survived that situation.

So, I reached out to my friend to ask how to write an appropriate trigger warning. I haven't lived through that situation myself. I don't really know how to care for those who have. Truthfully, if I didn't know my friend, I probably wouldn't have thought twice about sharing the video.

But, thankfully, I do know them, and I've been listening to their perspective for a while now. While I always strive to be kind in digital spaces – I don't do it perfectly, and I certainly don't have a tremendous amount of experience caring for trauma survivors. Knowing this remarkable person has helped me better understand how to be mindful of digital content that may be harmless for most, but is painful or traumatizing for others.

Turns out, they hadn't seen the video yet. My question about an appropriate trigger warning alerted them that the video probably contained something they might prefer not to see. If I hadn't asked, they might have clicked the video entirely unaware of what it contained.

If I had shared the video without asking, they might have clicked the video unaware *because of me*.

I'm deeply thankful that didn't happen. To understand why, read my friend's thoughts on the video at laurieworks.com, *How to Respect Gun Violence Survivors on Social Media*.

Please don't see this as a criticism of anyone who has shared or will share content like this. Rather, read it as a call to reflection and thoughtfulness about how our digital activity impacts the sea of people who encounter our posts.

Knowing someone who has lived through something we can hardly even imagine changes the way we think about those experiences and situations. Social media allows us to connect with and learn from people with vastly different experiences from our own. Digital kindness uses social media to connect with people on a deeper level, instead of sharing momentary shocks, laughs, and tears.

The more people we know and love, the more mindful we should be.

Digital kindness strives to unite not divide. It refrains from posting things that cause division, hurt, anger, and frustration. It considers the perspectives of others, the implications and what it says and does, and the potential impact of every post on anyone who might encounter it.

Digital kindness works toward compassion, understanding, and unity. When we use social media to get to know people, mindful posting will start to come naturally.

Chapter 5 Questions

- Do you speak differently one-on-one than you do when speaking to several people at once? How?

- What topics or types of content bother you in digital spaces? Do you ever post about these topics or post these types of content yourself?

- Has one of your posts been seen by someone you didn't intend to see it? What happened?

- Have you ever seen a post someone didn't intend for you to see? How did it make you feel?

- Has a friend or acquaintance posted something that hurt you or made you upset? How did you respond?

- Do you think before you post? What things do you think about?

Chapter 5 Activities

- On a holiday or on a day when a potentially difficult topic is trending, send a personal message to someone you know may be struggling with feelings related to the holiday or topic.

- Commit to *not* posting controversial content for a week. Evaluate your social media experience and feelings during that week.

- Before posting something controversial about a certain viewpoint or group of people, make an effort to ask the following questions:

- Do I *really* mean this? Do I really believe that anybody who holds that opinion is evil, stupid, or to blame for all the problems in the world?

- Am I certain *no one* I love, respect, and care about falls into the category of people I'm complaining about or criticizing?

- What if someone I love, respect, and care about *does* fall into a category of people I'm criticizing? How will my post make them feel? How might they choose to respond?

- Will I be surprised, hurt, or angry if someone decides to unfriend me, argue with me, or pull back from interacting with me because I posted a strong statement about people who hold views different from my own?

- Why am I posting this? What am I trying to accomplish?

6
KINDNESS IS HONEST

The ability to glimpse other people's lives through social media empowers us to gain a deeper and more thorough understanding of our fellow human beings ... especially those with lives vastly different from our own. Unfortunately, it also allows us to compare our lives, experiences, and accomplishments with those we consider peers.

More often than not, when people choose to use social media to compare themselves to others, they tend to find their own life lacking. A study conducted in 2014 by researchers at the University of Pittsburgh School of Medicine found that exposure to "highly idealized representations of peers on social media elicits feelings of envy and the distorted belief that others lead happier, more successful lives."

Our social media highlights have the potential to make others feel less accomplished, less popular, less happy, less healthy, less adequate in a million different ways.

Have you ever felt dissatisfied, frustrated, or unaccomplished while scrolling through your social media feeds? Does that feeling lead you to present a rosier picture of your life? Or does it inspire you to be more honest when posting in digital spaces? Digital kindness encompasses a willingness to reveal some of the difficult, less-than-perfect truths about our lives.

Being honest about the struggles we face and being willing to share mundane, unglamorous moments gives others a better sense of our whole and real lives. Just as we can use social media to truly see others, we can also allow others to truly see us. When we let others glimpse the real us — in all our complicated, messy, imperfection — we let them know they're not inadequate or unworthy. We let them know they're not alone.

This isn't easy. Believe me, I know. I try very hard to practice what I preach in digital spaces, but when I'm feeling scared, confused, hurt, or raw, I tend to shut down and go silent on social media. When I'm feeling insecure, I post more than usual ... and heavily filter and edit those posts. I sometimes don't even realize I'm doing it until someone makes a comment that alerts me to the changes in my own digital behavior. (Then I obsess about it endlessly, because I want to be a shining example of digital kindness, and I worry about being publicly called out for my actions not matching my words.)

Being honest about our real lives and real selves makes a big difference in digital spaces, though. Whatever trials we've endured, there's someone out there who has faced the same hardship. Whatever we're going through at the moment, there's another person dealing with the same thing. Our willingness to talk about our experiences opens the door to connecting with others facing similar situations. Sharing our stories may provide hope to those in despair. It may encourage someone to reach out for help and support. It may even help us find comfort, peace, and resolution ourselves.

Embracing transparency, honesty, and openness in our digital activity can be scary, but it can also lead to profound and important change. When we've taken the time to see, connect, listen, and thoughtfully communicate with others, they will find our experiences moving, relevant, and impactful. Our words will carry far more weight than words of people they don't "know".

For a long time, claims of racism and disparate treatment of minorities by law enforcement and the criminal justice system have been dismissed by large segments of our society. But as social media connects more and more people to communities different from their own, the pervasiveness and truth of these claims is becoming harder and harder to dismiss.

In the wake of several fatal police shootings of unarmed black men and women, a friend of mine used Facebook to share some of his experiences as a black man in America. He laid out his experiences with law enforcement, both negative and positive. With openness and vulnerability, he talked about his reactions to the news of yet another death:

I felt hate. I felt rage.... I felt pain. I felt grief. But more than anything else I felt fear. Not for myself, but for the future.... I wanted to share with the people who know me, why it has affected me so deeply. How it ties into my own scars. Why it feels so painful. Why it elicits temptation to hate. I also wanted you to know that I don't — and won't — entertain those things ....

I am posting MY experience, because I have a suspicion that my story is far more common than not.... I post my experience so that you know it's closer to home than you think. And that love, prayer, deeper involvement with one another, and forgiveness are the best options we have moving forward.

I won't submit to my fear, or my hate. I hope you will stand with me.

As a pastor it can't have been easy for him to publicly admit feelings of hate and rage. But vulnerability, transparency, and a commitment to sharing a full truth made his words all the more credible. He let people see his scars and his heart, and it opened the eyes of many who haven't lived the same reality. The post was received with gratitude, love, grief, and expressions of support.

Interestingly, another friend's Facebook post about his encounter with law enforcement was not as generously received. The post talked about how he, as a white man, had been let off with a warning when stopped for driving well over the speed limit. He intended it as an example of bias in law enforcement, but the post went beyond a mere description of his experience. It also opined about the awfulness of police officers and overreaches of the police state. Instead of contemplating the implications of his *experience* (that disparate treatment of whites versus minorities by law enforcement does happen), people responded to — and argued with — his *opinions* about law enforcement.

Thoughtful and honest posts about painful experiences, difficult situations, and the impact of intolerance have more power to open eyes than any manifesto, proclamation, or position statement. It's easy to find flaws or errors in an idea or an opinion. But it's hard to dismiss outright the true stories of real people. Whatever the issue, live-streaming, live-tweeting, and first-person accounts shared in digital spaces allow doubters and skeptics to walk a mile in someone else's shoes.

Sharing our experiences puts a human face on abstract concepts. It reminds everyone that real lives are impacted by events, ideas, rhetoric, policies, doctrines, laws, positions, and decisions. Telling our story can teach people how to support and care for those facing the same circumstances we've endured. It can also help others facing similar circumstances find resources and support.

Laurie Works is a mass shooting survivor using social media to help the world understand how to support a victim of a mass shooting ... and to demonstrate how many people every mass shooting affects. Whenever another shooting makes the news (unfortunately, an all too common event), Laurie talks about their experience and shares their insightful article *Supporting Victims of a Mass Shooting* (archived at laurieworks.com).

This digital activity makes a difference. People who have read Laurie's social media posts and articles are thinking twice about posting content that could cause mental anguish to a survivor. When they see others posting problematic content, they share Laurie's posts and articles to help increase awareness of how to care for victims.

Slowly but surely, Laurie's voice is being amplified by those they interact with in digital spaces. It's a voice that needs to be heard and deserves to be listened to. Laurie is a beacon of compassion, care, hope, and resilience — and they reach more people every day because of a willingness to share difficult personal truth on social media.

Laurie's reality is so very different from my own, but their experiences have become part of my perspective. As I ponder issues like mental health, gun control, and media coverage of tragedies, Laurie's voice is part of my thought process.

It can be scary to share our truth publicly. But there is real power in revealing the fullness of our lives. It softens hearts. Changes minds. Gives hope to those who feel alone, afraid, or helpless. Instead of feeds teeming with perfect photos and triumphant moments, honesty fills feeds with posts that say:

I hear you.
I see you.
I get it.
I've been there.
You're not alone.
Here are some things that help.

Here are some resources to check out.
Let's walk side by side together through this ordeal.

Of course, in pursing honesty and transparency in digital spaces, we can't forget about being thoughtful as well. Our lives are endlessly intertwined with other human beings, who may or may not be comfortable with having their truth exposed publicly. Before identifying someone by name, consider whether they'd be okay with the content of the post. When in doubt, ask them how they feel about being mentioned on social media in that context.

We can also tell our stories in general terms, without naming names or giving enough descriptive details for others to identify the people we are talking about. Names are rarely necessary in our storytelling. The details of what we're experiencing and how we're feeling can be shared without listing the entire cast of supporting characters.

Thoughtfulness is even more important when our experiences revolve around people who are easily identifiable even if we avoid naming or describing them. It's impossible to talk about spouses, children, parents, in-laws, siblings, bosses, and employees without someone having a good idea of exactly who we're discussing. When our truth is so closely intertwined with the stories of others, kindness dictates we give at least some consideration to their boundaries and wishes.

As I've said before, there are no right answers. Digital kindness in these circumstances manifests as a commitment to avoid posting rose-colored untruths. Broadcasting marital struggles is unkind to one's spouse, but it's unkind to others to post lovey-dovey status updates when a marriage is on the rocks. Dishonest posts contribute to the pervasive perception that everyone else's life is perfect and happy. Think of how different social media networks would look if we all refrained from being part of that vicious cycle.

When sharing our truth we must also be wary of falling into the trap of popularity or "viralness". Most of the time, transparency and honesty about our lives will resonate with only a few people at a time. Sometimes, though, our openness and vulnerability will strike a nerve. It's exciting to see people respond positively to our experiences. But it's tempting to tweak and modify our stories — or deliberately pick and choose which stories to tell — to increase likes, fans, shares, upvotes, and applause.

The pursuit of "instafame" on social media is treacherous. When we begin to filter and edit our real lives to resonate with more people, we become less real, less transparent, less whole, and less human. We are reduced from a complex and multi-faceted human being to one or two stories that become our identity. So, if you share your truth and find a chorus of affirmation, that's wonderful. But don't let that one truth become your sole defining characteristic. We're all so much more than one story, one experience, one characteristic ... and being honest about many aspects of our lives reveals that.

To people looking for genuine connection in digital spaces, one-note storytellers hold little appeal. An inspiring or compelling experience may grab attention initially, but if a person is only willing to talk about one topic, their posts soon become stale, repetitive, and hollow. Personally, the people who impact me most are those who share a variety of truths and experiences.

Ultimately, we must all make our own decisions about how much we're willing to reveal, who we're willing to identify, and what we hope to accomplish by sharing our truth. I tend to err on the side of not posting much about my painful and difficult experiences on social media. I already know I have a tendency to filter and edit when I'm feeling insecure, so I worry about the temptation to present an inauthentic version of my life. However, as I tell my own stories in one-on-one conversations and see how they impact other lives in positive ways, I am encouraged to share those stories in digital spaces where they can be amplified and reach even more people who might need to know they're not alone.

Being honest in digital spaces changes us and changes the people who encounter our stories. When we overcome our fear of sharing the truth about our less-than-perfect lives, the encouraging, loving, thankful responses we receive help combat any feelings of inadequacy or worthlessness we may harbor. Those who listen to the stories we share may discover they're not the only one facing a particular situation or they may become more aware of situations and experiences others face.

Digital kindness is honest — and that honesty leads to deeper connection and understanding.

Chapter 6 Questions

- Have you ever felt dissatisfied, frustrated, or unaccomplished while scrolling through your social media feeds? How does that feeling impact the types of things you post on social media? How does it impact the way you interact on social media?

- Have you ever used social media to talk about difficulties in your life? What did you talk about? What was the response?

- Have you ever been moved or impacted by someone else sharing about difficulties in their life via social media? Why did their post move or impact you?

- How do you distinguish between posts that are honest for the sake of opening up about difficult truths and posts that are primarily designed to get attention or "likes"?

Chapter 6 Activities

- Find two or three different posts about the same difficult subject. Write down how you each post makes you feel.

- Write a policy for how you will handle talking about difficult things in your life that involve others.

- Identify and write down experiences in your life where you felt alone and wished you knew of at least one person who had been through a similar experience. Think about whether others might be helped by hearing about your experience.

- Write about one experience where you felt alone. Consider sharing your experience on social media. Journal about how the thought of sharing makes you feel.

7

BEING KIND TO YOURSELF IN DIGITAL SPACES

When we consciously practice being more kind to others, we may find ourselves the center of many connections — a hub for kind interactions in the social media spaces we regularly frequent. People are drawn to those who make them feel comfortable, welcome, worthy, and safe.

Becoming more connected in an already hyper-connected world can take its toll on even the most people-centric person. When pursuing a path of conscious digital kindness, it's important to establish the practice of being kind to yourself to in digital spaces as well.

To be kind to ourselves, we have to be wise and discerning about how the digital world operates and how it interacts with and impacts the "real" world. We must also be aware of how our digital activity impacts our emotional and physical well-being. Finally, we have to find our own unique balance of engaging kindly with others and checking in with our own needs.

Be Savvy

As we work toward more purposeful and kind interactions in digital spaces, it's important to remember that most people we encounter aren't thinking about their own digital activity in strategic and intentional ways. The vast majority of people have no deliberate approach to what they post, when, or why.

People share articles because the headline caught their attention. They post photos because they liked the way they looked or they wanted other people to know about an experience they were having. They write manifestos about controversial issues because they want to be heard in that exact moment. They lament when they are sad or hurt or struggling with depression, fear, anxiety.

Because there's no generally agreed upon etiquette for behavior in digital spaces, most social media activity is spontaneous and reactionary.

When people *do* think about what they're posting, they often choose to post idealized versions of their life or one-sided arguments and examples that "prove" they're "right" about various topics and issues. Sometimes this is because they are trying to convince themselves that everything is okay in their own life. Sometimes they're trying to convince others to see things a certain way. Regardless of their reasoning, hardly anyone is thinking about the impact their posts will have on *you* or others. They're thinking about themselves.

Reminding yourself that people either aren't thinking

about their posts ... or are thinking about how it makes *them* look (not about how it will make *you* feel) can help you interpret and filter the barrage of messages you see every day.

In a Forbes article, Cara Friedman, Social Media Manager of ClassPass said "I certainly post things that will show off the best version of myself, and I know that when I see others through my feeds, they are likely doing the same. You shouldn't feel less confident or proud in your own accomplishments based on what you see others post. Remember, if you're not sharing your whole self on social media, others likely aren't either."

While most people aren't thinking strategically about their social media image or posting habits and the impact they have on those who follow them, we can't ignore the fact that are loads of people looking to make a sale, make a living, or "make it big" with their side business, writing, photography, influence, etc. These folks intentionally present a highly filtered and curated (sometimes even a completely false or fake) social media image. Worse yet, they often do it while claiming to be living "authentically".

These people strategically "perform" their "life" to convince others to buy products, become fans of their creations, or look to them as sources of wisdom or inspiration. They claim they are "being themselves" and often prove their "realness" by sharing vulnerable, painful, or messy parts of their lives — all while impeccably dressed, beautifully photographed, and poetically expressing their thoughts.

When encountering these types of posts or people, it's helpful to think about what is going on "behind-the-scenes."

How did they manage to capture a perfectly lit photo of their effortless, shy smile and casually tousled hair while peeking playfully from behind a rustic door at an abandoned farmhouse? Who is following them around taking moody, black and white photos as they wander pensively through the woods? How long did it take them to set up the camera and find the right angle to record video of that epic deadlift?

What are they leaving out of the well-written, self-reflective stories and thoughts they post? What unflattering facts and experiences are they glossing over, hiding, or avoiding in order to maintain the image and narrative they want to convey?

Most people don't have a skilled photographer following them around everywhere. Most people don't record their workouts every day then edit them down to a few key seconds to share on social media. Most people don't share their innermost thoughts or dispense wisdom and advice via social media on a routine basis.

Sure, we may occasionally spend some time trying to find the perfect angle for a photo, shooting some video of our accomplishments, or sharing a few thoughts on a subject … but we don't do it all the time — or with the goal of getting people to buy things or follow us.

Deliberate performance is not "real life" for most folks.

Likewise, most people don't think about a single topic or issue as incessantly as their social media posts may indicate. Unless they have some special expertise or knowledge, there's no reason to worry about the things they choose to post or take their perspective too seriously.

In the interest of honesty and transparency, all of this

applies to me. As "real" as I strive to be, I'm picking and choosing the parts of my life I reveal in digital spaces and in this book. I'm strategic about what I post. I edit my words. I select photos of myself that I find flattering. I struggle with how to share my authentic self when every social media interaction is a conscious and deliberate choice about what I'm putting out there.

Be Self-Aware

In addition to being savvy about the kinds of things people post and the reasons they post them, we can exercise self-care by being aware of how we feel when messages cross our feed, how we are interpreting messages, and how we feel when interacting with others in digital spaces.

When I was going through my divorce, I started to notice that "happy family" photos were really bothering me — on holidays. At first, I wanted to dismiss my feelings. I try not to compare myself to others, and I felt I *should be happy* when seeing happy photos of my friends. I didn't want to be a person who reacted negatively to the happiness of others. But the fact remained that those photos deeply impacted me.

Fear, sadness, depression, unworthiness, anxiety and insecurity are all feelings people report experiencing when consuming social media posts. Interestingly, many recent studies suggest the impact of social media on our feelings, moods, and perceptions has more to do with how we are already feeling when we consume social media than with the content of the posts we consume. I was already feeling sad about my divorce when consuming "happy family" photos on social media. It makes sense those photos would amplify my feelings of loss and grief.

Research suggests *anger* is the emotion most powerfully amplified by social media. Unfortunately, people say a lot of outrageous, insensitive, inflammatory, and downright rude things in digital spaces. Without the visual cues a person sends when connecting face to face, many social media users push the boundaries of civility and common decency farther than they ever would when sharing similar thoughts or ideas in person.

Posts about politics, religion, or controversial issues are some of the most rage-inducing content on social media. When people dismiss or attack our views — even without mentioning us directly — it can feel like a personal slight. The urge to respond, defend, and defeat may be strong.

We can take note of the types of content that consistently evokes strong emotions, reactions, or a compulsion to respond.

Not all social media posts create negative emotions, of course. Posts can be uplifting, inspirational, educational, and beautiful as well. Focusing our attention on content that connects us or make us feel seen, heard, understood and loved can help us navigate digital spaces in healthy ways as well.

Aside from our immediate reaction to various kinds of content, we can also be aware of how we interpret the messages we see. As we discussed in *Chapter 5: Kindness is Thoughtful,* lack of context (and unintended context) in digital spaces often leads to misunderstandings and misinterpretations. Digital communication often lacks the clues necessary to allow us to accurately interpret what others truly mean. When posts are vague or don't clearly identify the person or issue being talked about it, it's all too easy to read the post through our own lens — and assume it is directed at us.

If I see a post from a friend complaining about how no one cares about her, I immediately think, "Oh no! She's talking about me! I've failed her!" That's just the way my brain is wired. When I take a moment to consider my reaction, I realize it's highly unlikely she's talking about me. More importantly, if she is, a vague and broadly-worded social media post is not an appropriate way to engage with a friend.

Being aware of our own psychological filters and tendencies when we encounter social media posts can help us reevaluate our instinctive interpretations. Digital media is a mass broadcasting tool. Every post goes to lots and lots of people. Unless we are tagged or named in a post, it is more than reasonable to assume it has nothing to do with us.

If there are multiple ways to interpret a post, we can train ourselves to consider (and accept) positive interpretations instead of negative ones. It's usually pretty obvious when someone is intentionally being mean or belligerent. If the intent or tone is unclear, we can choose to assume the best and move on with our day.

Finally, we can also become more aware of the way we feel when interacting in digital spaces. Do we feel the need to respond quickly? Do our fingers fly over the keys or jab frantically at the keypad? Does our pulse quicken and our breath get shallow? Do we find ourselves writing, proof-reading, erasing, and rewriting over and over before posting? Are we on the verge of tears? Or smiling and laughing?

If the exchange was happening in-person, how would we be conducting the conversation? Would we be enjoying ourselves? Laughing? Yelling? Agreeing to disagree? Or feeling the need to walk away?

Would we even be having this conversation if we were interacting in person?

Throughout this book I've identified and discussed many limitations and drawbacks to digital communication. However, the ability to gauge our feelings and our physiological responses to ideas, personalities, and various forms of content is one tremendous advantage of engaging in digital spaces. We don't always have time or feel safe enough to evaluate our feelings or reactions when dealing with someone face to face. Online interactions, on the other hand, allow us to take all the time we need to reflect on how we're feeling, research our responses, and refine our views. We don't have to respond to something immediately.

Find Your Balance

There's no "right" way to "do" digital media on a personal level. Being kind to ourselves in digital spaces is all about developing approaches that help us feel positive and healthy in our digital consumption and interaction.

When we become aware of negative or "less than" feelings about our real lives whenever we come across highly curated performative posts — or when we find ourselves experiencing strong negative emotions when consuming certain types of content — some possible strategies include:

- Checking in with ourselves about our mood and our feelings before scrolling through social media feeds – how we feel *before* we view posts can impact how those posts make us feel.

- Having real life conversations with people whose lives appear perfect on social media channels or who espouse strong, unnuanced views on topics that matter to us. Chances are we'll discover their real life isn't as perfect or satisfying as the highlight reel we're seeing, or we'll discover their views aren't quite as rigid as they appear to be, or we'll gain a better understanding of why they think and post the way they do.

- Hiding or unfollowing people whose posts consistently make us feel insecure, unaccomplished, unfulfilled, "less than," angry, defensive, misunderstood, attacked, or dismissed.

- Deciding whether this is a person we need or want to be connected with on social media, and disconnecting from anyone we don't need or want in our digital landscape.

When I was reacting negatively to "happy family" photos, blocking or hiding them wasn't an option I wanted to explore because they were photos of people I cared about. My approach was to acknowledge my emotional reactions, using them as a springboard for processing some of my grief, anger, and despair at what was going on in my own life.

For the most part, that solution worked for me. One of my friends, on the other hand, chose to block/hide a few people she knew who were posting constantly about wedding preparations at a time when she was feeling particularly dissatisfied with her romantic life. She decided the posts were too constant and the people weren't important enough to her to continue to consume content that was impacting her sense of self-worth and positivity. That solution worked for her.

I repeat: *there's no right way to do this*. You get to take control of how you navigate digital spaces.

Other boundaries you may choose to set include:

- Limit the amount of time you spend on social media. You can do this by setting time limits and/or designating specific times of day when you'll check in on your social media feeds and times when you won't. Studies may indicate optimum time limits, but everyone is different. (I spend way more time on social media than many of my friends, but I also work in the field.) Experiment with limits that feel right to you.

- Train yourself to wait before responding to social media posts and messages. There's no reason you must respond right away ... and you may think and feel differently after mulling a post over for a while. Something that felt extremely urgent when you first saw it may not matter to you anymore after even a small period of time passes.

- Set your own terms of engagement. Decide which conversations you want to have on social media and which ones you'd rather avoid. Make a personal plan for dealing with ugly, hateful, angry posts. Ignore them? Report them? Call them out? When you decide ahead of time which people and topics you want to interact with, and how you want to handle uncivil, discourteous, disrespectful, or even tone-deaf or dismissive content, you'll be in control of your response instead of subject to the whim of whatever emotions the content creates.

- Use filters! Social networks are constantly changing how they deliver content and the options they provide users, so I won't get too technical here — but pretty much all of them provide ways to customize our experience. Some networks let you filter out posts and comments containing specific words. Some let you block or filter content you're not interested in seeing. Others let you report or flag content you find offensive.

As you already know, I'm not an advocate for tailoring social media consumption to deliberately create an echo chamber where we only encounter content we already agree with. But digital spaces can undoubtedly be hurtful, toxic, and detrimental to our social and emotional well-being. Being mindful of how we feel when interacting with digital media and developing approaches to caring for ourselves in digital spaces empowers us to embrace kindness to others and create a better digital world for everyone.

Chapter 7 Questions

- Is there one dominant feeling or emotion you tend to experience when navigating digital spaces? What is it? Is that feeling or emotion the same for every social network, or is it different depending on which network you're using?

- Have you noticed some types of content, topics, or people affecting you more negatively than others? What (or who) are they? Why do these affect you more negatively?

- Have you noticed some types of content, topics, or people affecting you more positively than others? What (or who) are they? Why do these affect you more positively?

- What are some topics or types of content you'd prefer to avoid on social media? Why?

- What are some topics or types of content you want to interact with on social media? Why?

Chapter 7 Activities

- For one day, track your activity in digital spaces. Note how much time you spend on social media, which networks you're using, how content and people impact you, what you choose to respond to, how you choose to respond, etc.

- Look for trends and themes in the digital activity you logged. Note anything that surprises you as well as anything you'd like to do differently.

- Create a personal plan for navigating digital spaces. Include any strategies or approaches you'd like to adopt in caring for yourself and being purposeful about your social media use.

LAUREN M. HUG

8
ADVOCATE FOR DIGITAL KINDNESS

Digital communication is a relatively new frontier in human interaction. It is still emerging and evolving — and we are evolving with it. We're all figuring out what it means to be human in a digital world. No one before us has tackled this question. No one before us had access to this type of instant communication, this mass of information, this constant stream of voices, images, messages, and conversations.

No one before us had to think about broadcasting on multiple mass channels — what to say, what to show, or what our posting choices might tell others about us and about themselves. It's complicated, to say the least.

We can't think through every consequence of every post. We can't always anticipate how someone will react, or how our posts will be perceived both now and in the future.

We can't prevent people from broadcasting moments of our lives or sharing things we trusted them to keep secret.

No matter how hard we may try, none of us are perfect.

We're going to post something we regret. We're going to say something without thinking. We're going to forget who is listening. We're going to be insensitive. Something will be publicly shared that we'd prefer have been kept private. It's going to happen to every one of us. Not even opting out of social media completely can prevent it, because everyone else in the world is walking around with cameras and broadcasting devices in the palm of their hands.

No matter how purposeful we are about our own digital conduct and interactions, we cannot fully control the stories and images that others circulate about us. Nor are we always capable of or comfortable with publicly sharing the context or circumstances that led to images or stories about us.

Because of that, we *all* need to be more mindful of the judgements we make and the things we say publicly when we see imperfect behavior in digital spaces. There are far too many stories about lives being ruined after one questionable post — without surrounding context or a thorough understanding of the actual human beings involved — was plastered across social networks.

Whatever you ultimately decide about your personal approach to navigating digital spaces, please think about the choices you are making and grant grace to yourself and others.

Every time we click something or share something, we're transmitting that image, article, opinion, event, or concept. But we have a *choice* about whether we transmit that or not. We can choose *what* we transmit.

And we can choose *how* we transmit it. We can choose to go overboard in communicating goodwill, assuming positive intent, and trying to find common ground ... instead of jumping to conclusions about people based on the little pieces of information we think we know about them.

Digital etiquette is still evolving, but we can choose to be front-runners of digital kindness. Through our use of social media to see, connect, and listen — and through our digital thoughtfulness and honesty — we can show others that social media can be positive, not negative. We can choose to use these technologies as a powerful force for good.

Digital media opens the world up to us. It gives us the ability to connect in ways we never have before and to meet people we would never otherwise meet. We have the opportunity to talk to people from all walks of life and all across the globe about the things that matter to them most.

When we look into other people's lives, we can see all the things we share in common. We can see the things that make us human. We can highlight the things that unite us instead of the things that divide us. We can build community across traditional boundaries. Strangers can become friends through a shared experience or a common goal.

Digital kindness reclaims digital spaces as *human* spaces.

In my hometown of Colorado Springs we have amazing sunrises and sunsets. Every time the sky turns brilliant shades of pink or orange or purple, all of social media is flooded with photos of this breathtaking beauty. EVERYONE in Colorado Springs shares sunrise and sunset photos. No matter who they are or where they come from, everyone is captivated by the natural beauty we all have the privilege of witnessing.

We all appreciate beauty. We hold that in common. Social media can remind us of that. It's something to build upon. It's a starting point for recognizing our shared humanity.

Digital kindness reminds us we're all human.

We never, never, never know exactly why people do what they do. But, if we're willing to grant grace, we may discover more about people. We can look at the bigger picture of their complete life (if we know them personally). We can look at the totality of their digital presence (if we only know them online). We can engage in genuine and respectful dialogue either in person or in digital spaces.

In January of 2019, comedian Patton Oswalt was the subject of some angry tweets. His response is a tremendous example of advocating for digital kindness.

"Aw, man," Oswalt tweeted. "This dude just attacked me on Twitter and I joked back but then I looked at his timeline and he's in a LOT of trouble health-wise. I'd be pissed off too."

By taking the time to look past the angry tweet, Oswalt acknowledged the humanity of his attacker — and the possibility that, when faced with similar circumstances, he might act out in the same way.

Oswalt did more than just acknowledge the man's humanity and difficulty of the circumstances he found himself in. Oswalt donated $2,000 to the man's crowdfunding campaign to cover medical expenses — and he urged all of his Twitter followers to do the same. That tweet led to donations totaling ten times more than the man's fundraising goal. One small act of kindness was amplified astronomically.

In an interview with the Washington Post, the man said he expected a scathing retort or to be ignored in response to his angry tweet. Oswalt's kindness was something he could never have imagined.

It completely changed the man's perspective.

In a follow up tweet he said, "[Patton Oswalt] not only let me slide on a rough tweet to him but started something that has me reevaluating friendships and productive dialogue regardless of political affiliation."

That's just one example.

Imagine the world we can create, if we all use digital interactions as opportunities to be kind!

Chapter 8 Questions

- Have you ever regretted anything you've posted or a way you've interacted in digital spaces? Why did you regret it? What would you do differently in the future?

- Do you believe you can change the world (or one small corner of it) by being kind in digital space? How so?

- Do you plan to advocate for digital kindness? If so, in what ways?

Chapter 8 Activities

- Review your social media activity for the past month. Identify activity you're proud of. Identify activity you regret or would like to do differently in the future.

- Find a post that made you angry. Take a deep breath, and respond in kindness. Note any reactions to your response.

A Closing Invitation ...

Throughout this book, I've offered lots of suggestions on how to approach behavior in digital spaces. My goal is to spark discussion and guide people toward more purposeful and meaningful use of digital technology. I don't have all the answers. Not all of my suggestions will work for everybody ... or in every situation. Tag me on Twitter (@LaurenHug) and let's talk about how we can all be more purposeful about our use of digital technology. Together we can create safer, healthier digital spaces ... and, ultimately, a better world.

ABOUT THE AUTHOR

An accomplished speaker, writer, and strategist, Lauren Hug combines communication and research theory with multi-way engagement methods to build and empower vibrant communities in both digital and physical spaces. For the past decade, she has applied analytical and communication skills to market research, presentation, and, increasingly, social media needs of businesses, big and small. As founder of HugSpeak Coaching, she relies on presentation experience from the courtroom to the boardroom, involvement with dozens of corporate campaigns, and cultural sensitivity from traveling and living abroad to advise clients in a wide variety of industries. Her positive, collaborative approach has been described as empowering, life-changing, and even therapeutic.

Lauren is an attorney and certified mediator whose academic credentials include an LL.M. with merit from University College London, a J.D. with honors from the University of Texas School of Law, and a Bachelor of Journalism and Bachelor of Arts in Spanish from the University of Texas. She is the author of *The Professional Woman's Guide to Getting Promoted (Packt 2015)* and *The Manager's Guide to Presentations* (Packt 2014). She lives in Colorado Springs, Colorado.

Made in the USA
Middletown, DE
23 July 2019